Academy Album

A Pictorial Selection of Works of Art in the Collections

Honolulu
Academy
of Arts

HONOLULU, HAWAII

Copyright 1968, Honolulu Academy of Arts
Published by Honolulu Academy of Arts
Printed by Edward Enterprises, Inc.
Honolulu, Hawaii, United States of America
Library of Congress Catalog Card No. 68-8958

Introduction

Works of art are enduring records of mankind linking the yesterdays with the todays and tomorrows. As manifestations of man's evolving thought and activity, they provide insight to his creative nature as well as his history. Art informs, stimulates and gives pleasure; it has significant influence on our daily lives.

Such convictions as these motivated Mrs. Charles Montague Cooke to share her interest in art with her community, and she consequently founded and initially endowed the Honolulu Academy of Arts, which first opened to the public in 1927. Encouraged and aided by her family and friends, Mrs. Cooke gave Hawaii its major art center, in fact the only art museum of a broad general nature in the Pacific. A tax free institution governed by a board of trustees, the Academy over the years has acquired a justifiable reputation abroad for a notable collection housed in one of the most beautiful buildings of its kind.

This publication offers a pictorial review of more than 100 noteworthy objects selected from the broad range of Academy holdings. Organized by cultural division and historical sequence, each picture section provides information on the general content and features of a particular area of the collections. Decorative arts are not specifically treated here, but they are indicated in section comments and in certain gallery views. As reflected in the following pages, the museum's main strength lies in the collections of oriental arts, significantly those of China, Japan and Korea. Altogether, Academy holdings—developed around Mrs. Cooke's collection—are richly diverse and represent creative achievements in many parts of the world, spanning ancient times to the present.

The Academy is not only a repository, and something more of its story needs to be told in brief. Serving the community as a source of knowledge and inspiration, it is fundamentally an educational institution, as projected in the words of the opening dedication:

"That our children of many nationalities and races, born far from the centers of art, may receive an intimation of their own cultural legacy and wake to the ideals embodied in the arts of their neighbors, that they may grasp that composite heritage accumulating for the new generations of Hawaii;

"That Hawaiians, Americans, Chinese, Japanese, Koreans, Filipinos, North Europeans, South Europeans and all other people living here, contacting through the channel of art those deep intuitions common to all, may perceive a foundation on which a new culture, enriched by all the old strains, may be built in these Islands;

"That it may contribute to such understanding and mutual respect, the Honolulu Academy of Arts will open its doors to this community, so situated that it calls East the West and West the East, perhaps in happy continuance of that ancient Polynesian custom of exchanging the names of close friends."

Now that the State of Hawaii has become virtually a link between East and West, with an attendant influx of peoples and ideas, the founder's intentions for the Academy have taken on added dimensions. Thus the program is geared to an expanding range of interests which further demonstrate the nature of the visual arts as an international language of expression.

The gracious setting in which the Academy functions occupies an entire city block, the original building having been designed by the firm of Bertram G. Goodhue Associates of New York. With its steeply pitched tile roof and stuccoed stone structure, it reflects influences from the Mediterranean and the Orient as well as from Polynesia, providing an effect that is distinctively suitable for its location and use.

Making possible a dual emphasis on East and West, the building provides, on one side, a series of galleries for the far eastern arts, with access to an inviting oriental garden court; on the other side similar areas, with a Spanish courtyard, serve to present the arts of the West. Such a plan allows installations suggestive of the objects' origins in the context of time and place. Out of public view and below the main gallery level are work areas and a number of storage vaults with many additional art objects—paintings, graphics, textiles, ceramics, lacquer, Japanese screens, etc.—some of which are exhibited in rotation, while others are held for study purposes.

The C. Montague Cooke Jr. graphic arts galleries—which permit a variety of exhibitions drawn from the museum's collection of prints and drawings—are approached from yet another open court. Still further gallery space is located on the second floor, used for presentations of the Academy's contemporary collection and for special exhibitions which regularly augment the permanent installations. Here the Artists of Hawaii annual exhibition is held each fall, as well as featured showings of work by local painters, sculptors and craftsmen.

From time to time the Academy's exhibition program has included major presentations of national treasures, such as those sponsored by the governments of Japan, Korea, Thailand, India and Iran. Also, loan shows of both historical and contemporary significance are brought from mainland sources to provide a wide range of art experience.

Available to scholars and Academy Members as well as serving the professional needs of the staff, the Academy's art reference library houses some 18,000 volumes, with notable strength in the oriental field. The three story library wing (1956) was given by the late Robert Allerton, whose lifetime contributions and subsequent bequest have greatly enriched the museum's overall development.

Another three story addition (1960), with its own fountain courtyard, is devoted entirely to educational activities. Extensive space on two levels provides lecture galleries and creative studios for a broadly conceived young people's program conducted by the Academy's education department. Having liaison with the public school system and drawing on private schools as well, the department has almost a year-round schedule of events—often tying in with classroom studies—bringing thousands of children into the Academy annually. Many more are reached through out-service activities. The program not only acquaints Hawaii's young people with the achievements of artists throughout the ages but also emphasizes the importance of creative activity in the development of the individual. In addition, attention is given to the needs of school art teachers, for whom conferences and workshops are scheduled regularly.

For creative instruction on the adult level, the upper floor of the education wing affords excellent facilities for the Studio Program, concentrated in the disciplines of painting, drawing and commercial art. The yearly appointment of a Resident Artist gives opportunity for study with a succession of prominent painters from art centers beyond Hawaii. Limited enrollment permits individualized supervision for those interested in career opportunities, and special classes are also offered to Academy Members seeking creative fulfillment through art expression.

A large and growing membership body is an important aspect of community involvement in the Academy's program. Apart from their contributions to the institution's financial well-being, Members of the Academy enjoy special opportunities offered through lectures, demonstrations, exhibition previews and receptions, museum publications, performances of related arts, various entertainments, etc. Benefits include discounts on purchases from the Academy Shop, which offers the largest selection of art books in Honolulu and also stocks reproductions of paintings, sculpture and jewelry.

In a continuing state of growth, the Academy is beholden to its many supporters whose interest and generosity assure its development. It is unfortunately not possible to record here all those who have helped the museum to reach its present stature. In addition to the few individuals noted by reason of their marked influence on the collections, many others have contributed time, effort, thought and gifts which have benefited the total program. To all of these benefactors, this Album is dedicated with lasting appreciation.

JAMES W. FOSTER, JR. *Director*

Grateful acknowledgement is due Academy staff members who participated in the preparation of this book, with special recognition of the contributions of Lewis W. Story, Assistant Director; Robert P. Griffing, Jr., Curatorial Consultant; Joseph Feher, Curator of Graphic Arts and Designer of Publications; Leslie B. Nerio, Assistant Curator of Oriental Arts, and Raymond Sato, Photographer.

J. W. F.

European
and
American
Collections

European and American Collections

The European and American collections of the Academy provide a broad sampling of western art developments and in numerous instances offer viewing experiences of a high aesthetic order. Recent years have seen the addition of a diversified number of works ranging in date from the first years of the Christian era to the present time. Further acquisitions are actively sought in a continuing effort to provide a more cohesive experience, historically and aesthetically, for the Academy audience.

An abbreviated account of the development of the Academy's occidental collection is given in the following paragraphs. "Named" collections are briefly described, with the recognition that there have been many other substantial contributions less formally identifiable.

The Robert Allerton Collection comprises a vast array of objects which are to be found in almost every exhibition area of the Academy. Many of these pieces were presented by Mr. Allerton during his lifetime, others are purchases from the Allerton Acquisition Fund, and still others have been acquired as memorials. The Wilhelmina Tenney Memorial Fund also has been a source through which the collections have been monumentally enriched.

In 1961 the Samuel H. Kress Foundation, as a part of its nationwide program of art patronage, presented the Academy with a collection of sixteen Italian paintings representing important artists of the Renaissance period. These are displayed, as is often the case in Academy installations, with sculpture and examples of the decorative arts.

Soon after the Academy opened its doors, the textile department received the Henrietta Brewer Collection of Mediterranean Textiles which provided an impetus for later developments. In 1951 the Blanche R. Mandel Collection, comprised of a remarkable group of 17th to 19th century European laces, was presented by Mr. and Mrs. Fred L. Mandel, Jr.

One of the strongest departments in the Academy is that of prints and drawings. The collection was started upon the Academy's inauguration by a large gift of prints belonging to Dr. and Mrs. C. Montague Cooke, Jr. The income from a fund established after Dr. Cooke's death in 1948 has allowed for a continuing program of important purchases. Prints and drawings from many other sources are also included, and the outstanding collection of Japanese woodblock prints is discussed in the section dealing with oriental art.

The Friends of the Academy, an organization active in the 1940's under the leadership of Mrs. Walter F. Dillingham, Mrs. Philip E. Spalding and Mr. Robert Allerton, was instrumental in the acquisition of important works by French and American artists of the late 19th and early 20th centuries. Mrs. Carter Galt added significantly to the representation of the Post-Impressionist School with excellent works by Vlaminck and Modigliani. The Watumull Foundation has been a consistent contributor in the area of contemporary Hawaiian art, and examples by recognized modern American and European artists are accumulating through the generosity of Joseph H. Hazen, the late Stanley Barbee and other donors.

Ancient Mediterranean

The area of Mediterranean antiquities has not been one of primary interest and collecting activity. The objects illustrated, along with twenty or so additional examples, are largely thought of as a modest educational resource. To supplement the permanent installation, the yearly schedule of temporary exhibitions organized by the education department usually includes "The Ancient World," which treats with the same area and is drawn from material in the reserve collections.

In addition to the objects illustrated, the collection includes several relief fragments from a Roman sarcophagus; a fine alabaster urn (formerly in the collection of the descendants of Prince Caffarelli in Naples) from the excavations at Herculaneum; a mosaic from Daphne, near Antioch; examples of various Greek pottery shapes and styles; a group of three Tanagra figurines and a fragmentary marble head of Athena from the 4th century B.C. An important gift in 1966 was the Kayyem Collection of Roman Glass, made up of a wide range of types, primarily from sites in the Near East. This material, along with examples previously in the collection, offers an impressive representation of late Roman glass production.

Coptic textile (detail)

PORTRAIT OF A MAN AND HIS WIFE
Egyptian, late 5th Dynasty, c. 2500 B.C.
limestone, 20" high
Purchase, 1938
4704

STANDING FIGURE OF PHARAOH
Egyptian, late 5th Dynasty, c. 2500 B.C.
limestone relief from a tomb in Sakkara, 63" high
Gift of Mrs. Charles M. Cooke, 1930
2896

14

HEAD OF A MAN
Assyrian, 7th century B.C.
marble relief from the palace of
Sargon at Khorsabad, 16" high
3607

BLACK FIGURED AMPHORA
Greek, mid-5th century B.C.
ceramic with painted decoration, 10½" high
Gift of Mrs. Charles M. Cooke, 1930
2891

SEATED AND STANDING IBIS
Egyptian, c. 4th century B.C.
wood and bronze, 12½" and 16" high
Purchases, 1954
2003.1 and 2004.1

HEAD OF ATHENA
Greek, c. 400 B.C.
marble, 11½" high
Gift of Mrs. Charles M. Cooke, 1933
3604

Medieval and Early Renaissance

In addition to the illustrated stone Madonna and Child (page 23) are a smaller and slightly earlier piece of the same subject, probably from Normandy, and a limestone St. Michael and the Dragon, dating from the 15th century. The School of Avignon is represented by a large polychrome wood figure of St. John the Evangelist. Important panel paintings of the period include: "The Holy Family" by Albert Bouts; "The Presentation of the Virgin" by Andrea di Bartolo; a Vivarini, "Madonna and Child," and a work of the same subject attributed to the Master of San Miniato. "The Adoration of the Magi" attributed to the Master of 1518 (page 25) was originally the central panel of a five part altarpiece, other panels of which are now in the National Gallery, London, and the Museum Meyer van der Bergh, Brussels. Exhibited with the ivory (page 21) and a Limoges enamel reliquary are two illuminated pages from a Book of Hours, and the German stained glass, "Flight into Egypt" (page 22), is shown with a second piece of the same origin. The gallery in which these works are displayed also contains examples of French Gothic and early Italian Renaissance furniture.

Graphic works in the collection include fine impressions of Durer, van Leyden and Schongauer and an important drawing with water-color by Hoefnagel. These works, along with others, are periodically shown in thematic exhibitions in the C. Montague Cooke Jr. graphic arts galleries.

Flemish tapestry (detail)

WORKSHOP OF ORCAGNA
Italian, c. 1308-1369
Triptych of the Madonna and Child with Saints, 1391
tempera on panels
center: 53¾" x 27", sides: 49" x 24"
Gift of Mrs. Charles M. Cooke, 1928
2834

CRUCIFIXION
French, c. 1400
ivory, 3¾" x 3⅜"
Gift of Mr. and
Mrs. Livingston Jenks, 1961
2887.1

ARCHITECTURAL DECORATION—
A CHURCH AND TWO FIGURES
French, 14th century
limestone relief,
probably from a capital, 15½" high
Purchase, 1949
905.1

THE FLIGHT INTO EGYPT
probably German, 14th century
stained glass, 20½" x 18¼"
Purchase, 1934
4055

VIRGIN AND CHILD
French (Burgundian), 15th century
limestone, 57" high
The Robert Allerton Fund, 1956
2254.1

QUEEN SEMIRAMIS OF BABYLON WITH ATTENDANTS
Flemish (made at Tournai), c. 1480
wool and silk millefleurs tapestry, 99¼" x 102"
Gift of the Charles M. and Anna C. Cooke Trust, 1946
325.1

ATTRIBUTED TO THE MASTER OF 1518
Flemish (Antwerp)
Adoration of the Magi
oil on panel, 32" x 27⅝"
Purchase, 1963
3103.1

24

Italian Renaissance

Gifts from the Samuel H. Kress Foundation which should be noted in addition to those works illustrated are: Two Apostles, panels originally part of the predella of an altarpiece which Carlo Crivelli painted for the church of the Franciscan friars in Montefiore dell-Aso near Ascoli Piceno; a Madonna and Child by Segna de Bonaventura; Four Male Saints from the studio of Fra Filippo Lippi, thought to be from the great altarpiece of S. Trainita in Pistoia; "Madonna Adoring the Child" by Pintoricchio and "Bust Portrait of a Young Man," a masterly example of Salviati's portraiture.

Sculpture of the period is not extensively represented. In addition to the Antonio Rossellino illustrated ("St. John the Baptist," page 28) is a second work by the same artist, "Madonna and Child with Angels," a polychrome stucco bas-relief, and a polychrome terracotta bust portrait of a young man. The author of this last work, undoubtedly a Florentine who probably worked in the circle of Donatello, has not been identified. Furniture and decorative arts in the gallery installations include a 15th century cassone, an early 16th century writing desk and a fine gilded silver tazza or footed cup from Portugal.

27

Embroidered vestment (detail)

ANDREA MANTEGNA
1431-1506
Bacchanalian Group with Wine Press
engraving, 11⅞" x 17½"
Purchase,
C. Montague Cooke Jr. Fund, 1951
13,069

PIERO DI COSIMO
Florentine School, 1462?-1521
Saint John the Evangelist
oil on panel, 32¾ x 23¼"
Samuel H. Kress Collection, 1961
2989.1

ANTONIO ROSSELLINO
Florentine School, 1427?-1479?
Saint John the Baptist
terracotta, 13½" high
The Wilhelmina Tenney
Memorial Fund, 1957
2298.1

FRANCESCO GRANACCI
Florentine School, 1469-1543
Adoration of the Christ Child
tondo painted on panel, diameter: 34½"
Samuel H. Kress Collection, 1961
2987.1

30

DOMINICO CAMPAGNOLA
1484-1550
Landscape
sepia, 11¾" x 17½"
Purchase, C. Montague Cooke Jr. Fund, 1957
13,927

GIOVANNI BATTISTA MORONI
School of Bergamo, c. 1520-1578
Portrait of a Man, 1553
oil on canvas, 41⅛" x 32⅜"
Samuel H. Kress Collection, 1961
2982.1

PAOLO CALIARI called "IL VERONESE"
Venetian School, 1528-1588
The Descent from the Cross, c. 1565
oil on canvas, 15⅞" x 14"
Samuel H. Kress Collection, 1961
2990.1

17th, 18th and 19th Centuries

The collections are largely comprised of works from England, Italy, France and America and are generally shown according to these national identifications. Falling outside this general plan are a number of exceptions, including the "Portrait of David de Ruyter" by the Dutchman, Jan Anthonisz van Ravesteyn; an 18th century terracotta sculpture of "St. Michael Overcoming the Forces of Evil" from Austria or South Germany, and watercolors by the Russian artist, Louis Choris, who accompanied the Russian Imperial Navy expedition to Polynesia during the early 19th century (page 46). The installations incorporate furniture, porcelains, glass and other types of decorative arts. Outstanding in this body of 18th century material are a Venetian desk with decoupage decoration, a set of four French trophy carvings, a wide range of English furniture styles from the Lily Love Cooke Memorial Collection, a Waterford crystal chandelier and an inlaid mahogany Hepplewhite sideboard made in New York State.

The textile department is particularly rich in 17th to 19th century examples, most of which are reserved for special temporary showings. The two major holdings include Mediterranean textiles of the late 18th and 19th centuries and a remarkable group of European laces.

Paintings of interest, not shown in the following illustrations, include a Bonavia landscape (a companion piece to the work appearing on page 41), a pair of gouache landscapes by Marco Ricci, "Portrait of an Actress" by Sir Joshua Reynolds, and two Robert Dampier portraits of the children of the Hawaiian King, Kamehameha I. American works include a portrait of George Washington by Charles Wilson Peale, founder of the Peale family of artists and older brother of James Peale, whose still life is illustrated (page 45); small but fine examples by Harnett and Whistler, in addition to the latter's major portrait of Lady Meux (page 48), and a Venetian period work by Thomas Moran. The galleries also contain a marble bust of Daphne by Hiram Powers, a gilded weather vane in the form of an eagle, and a group of works by anonymous 19th century American artists.

French lace (detail)

36

ABRAHAM BLOMAERT
Dutch, 1564-1651
Personages in Elaborate Costumes
sepia, 12" x 8"
Purchase
C. Montague Cooke Jr. Fund, 1953
13,262

JAN ANTHONISZ VAN RAVESTEYN
Dutch, c. 1572-1657
Portrait of David de Ruyter, 1639
oil on panel, 40" x 29¼"
Purchase, 1966
3382.1

GUERCINO (GIOVANNI FRANCESCO BARBIERI)
Italian, 1591-1666
Landscape
sepia, 11" x 16⅝"
Purchase, 1951
12,977

ISAAC VAN OSTADE
Dutch, 1621-1649
Interior of a Dutch Farmhouse
ink and watercolor, 6⅛" x 6½"
Purchase,
C. Montague Cooke Jr. Fund, 1956
13,759

ALESSANDRO MAGNASCO
Italian, 1667-1749
Figures before a Stormy Sea
oil on canvas, 28¼" x 37½"
Purchase
Louise and Walter F. Dillingham Fund, 1964
3301.1

GIOVANNI PAOLO PANNINI
Italian, c. 1691-1765
Capriccio with Marcus Aurelius Statue and the Farnese Hercules
watercolor, 14" x 9½"
Purchase, Robert Allerton Fund, 1965
15,107

HUBERT ROBERT
French, 1733-1808
Landscape with Figures
sanguine, 16⅝" x 12½"
Purchase, C. Montague Cooke Jr. Fund, 1964
15,090

40

CARLO BONAVIA
Italian (Neapolitan School), active 1755-1788
Castel dell'Ovo, 1788
oil on canvas, 37¾'' x 47½''
Samuel H. Kress Collection, 1961
2991.1

ADELAIDE LABILLE-GUIARD
French, 1749-1803
Portrait of Monsieur Meunier, 1796
oil on canvas, 29" x 23½"
Purchase, 1962
3067.1

GILBERT STUART
American, 1755-1828
Portrait of Governor John Brooks, c. 1815
oil on panel, 32"x 26"
Given in memory of Mr. Edward T. Harrison, 1965
3370.1

42

FRANCISCO JOSE DE GOYA Y LUCIENTES
Spanish, 1746-1828
Los Chinchillas (from *Los Caprichos*), 1796-1798
aquatint, first edition, 6⅞" x 4⅞"
Purchase, 1938
11,121

43

SIR HENRY RAEBURN
English, 1756-1823
Portrait of the Countess of Aboyne
oil on canvas, 50" x 40"
Bequest of Mrs. Gayer C. Dominick
in memory of Mrs. Bayard Dominick, 1964
3296.1

JAMES PEALE
American, 1749-1831
Still Life, c. 1824
oil on panel, 18" x 26½"
Gift of Mrs. Edward T. Harrison, 1967
3497.1

LOUIS CHORIS
Russian, 1795-1828
Temple in the Sandwich Isles and
Women of the Sandwich Isles
watercolor and drawing, 6½" x 12" and 6½" x 9⅜"
Purchase, Honolulu Art Society, 1944
12,160

WALLPAPER WITH SCENES
BASED ON
THE PACIFIC VOYAGES OF
CAPTAIN COOK AND OTHERS (detail)
designed by J. C. Charvet and
printed in France between 1804-1806
woodblock, 20 panels, each 77" x 21"
Gift of Mrs. Charles M. Cooke, 1928
2692

46

EUGENE DELACROIX
French, 1798-1863
The Justice of Trajan, 1858
oil on canvas, 25" x 20¾"
Purchase, 1941
4954

WINSLOW HOMER
American, 1836-1910
Fisherwomen, Tynmouth, England, 1881
watercolor, 13½" x 19⅜"
Purchase, 1964
15,091

JAMES ABBOTT McNEILL WHISTLER
American, 1834-1903
Arrangement in Black No. Five: Lady Meux, 1881
oil on canvas, 76½" x 51¼"
Purchase, special Academy funds and
donations from the community, 1967
3490.1

49

PIERRE AUGUST RENOIR
French, 1841-1919
study for *Dance in the Country*
pencil, 19½" x 13¾"
Purchase, 1937
10,955

50

PAUL CEZANNE
French, 1839-1906
Portrait of a Man
pencil, 20" x 17¼"
Purchase, 1937
10,957

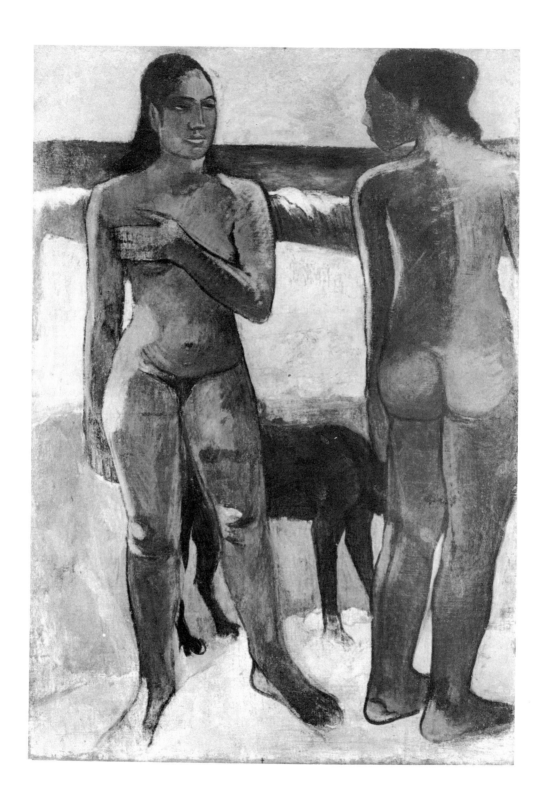

VINCENT VAN GOGH
Dutch, 1853-1890
Wheatfield, c. 1889
oil on canvas, 20¾" x 25¼"
Gift of Mrs. Richard A. Cooke and family
as a memorial to Mr. Richard A. Cooke, 1946
377.1

PAUL GAUGUIN
French, 1848-1903
Two Nudes on a Tahitian Beach, c. 1890
oil on canvas, 35¾" x 25½"
Gift of Mrs. Charles M. Cooke, 1933
3901

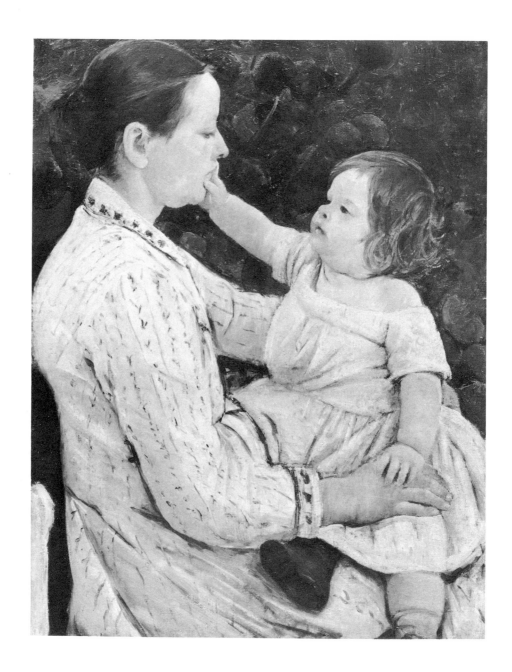

MARY CASSATT
American, 1845-1926
Maternal Caress, 1890-1895
oil on canvas, 26" x 21"
Given in memory of Miss Wilhelmina Tenney
by a group of her friends, 1953
1845.1

CAMILLE PISSARRO
French, 1830/31-1903
View of the Port of Rouen, 1898
oil on canvas, 25" x 31¼"
Gift of Mrs. Charles M. Cooke, 1934
4110

55

20th Century

Some important movements in the development of 20th century European and American art are represented by notable examples reproduced on the following pages. Continued effort is being made to strengthen and expand holdings of significance in our own time, with particular emphasis on influential directions in the United States. In reference to the latter and not illustrated, such masters as Stuart Davis, Maurer, Crawford, Demuth, Feininger, Pereira, Hofmann, Tobey, Guston and Francis, among others, are included. Fine works by Yunkers, Hultberg, Kanemitsu and Peterdi were acquired when each was Resident Artist in the program begun in 1965. Thomas Wilfred's innovative "lumia" composition should be especially noted, as well as a group of early works in bronze and marble by Nadelman.

The collection's modest but choice representation of the "School of Paris" includes, in addition to those illustrated, paintings by Picasso, Tanguy, Dufy, Redon, and Severini, with major canvases by Delaunay ("Arc-en-Ciel," 1913) and Ozenfant ("Abstract Composition," 1925). Sculpture by Maillol, Despiau, Moore and the fine head of Albert Einstein by Epstein give added dimension to the European holdings.

The collection of 20th century prints grows steadily more substantial through gifts as well as through a purchase program made possible by the C. Montague Cooke Jr. Fund established for this purpose. The schedule of temporary exhibitions for the graphic arts galleries draws alternately on material from the permanent collection and loan exhibitions from mainland and local collections.

Mention should also be made of the substantial representation of contemporary painting, sculpture and prints produced by artists of Hawaii.

57

Hans Hofmann painting (detail)

THOMAS EAKINS
American, 1844-1916
William Rush and his Model, 1907-1908
oil on canvas, 35¼" x 47¼"
Gift of the Friends of the Academy, 1947
548.1

58

MAURICE DE VLAMINCK
French, 1876-1958
The Alley, 1910
oil on canvas, 29" x 21½"
Gift of Mrs. Carter Galt, 1963
3173.1

CHILDE HASSAM
American, 1859-1935
Isle of Shoals, Broad Cove, 1911
oil on canvas, 36" x 34½"
Purchase and gift of
Mrs. Robert P. Griffing, Jr., and
Miss Renee Halbedl, 1964
3194.1

MAURICE BRAZIL PRENDERGAST
American, 1859-1924
Afternoon, Pincian Hill
watercolor, 15⅛" x 10⅝"
Gift of Mrs. Philip E. Spalding, 1940
11,653

60

EMIL ANTOINE BOURDELLE
French, 1861-1929
The Great Penelope,
first cast in 1912
bronze, cast number 4, 96" high
Given in memory of
Mrs. Richard A. Cooke
by her children, 1965
3334.1

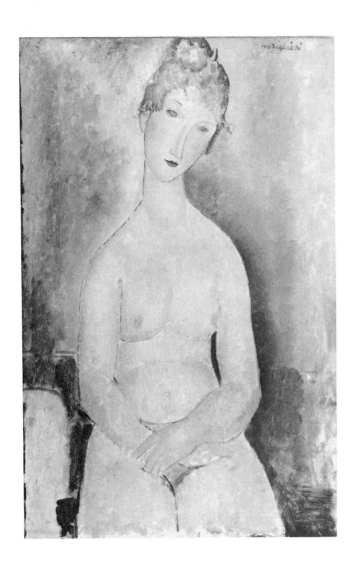

AMEDEO MODIGLIANI
Italian, 1884-1920
Seated Nude, c. 1918
oil on canvas, 39½" x 25½"
Gift of Mrs. Carter Galt, 1960
2895.1

JOHN MARIN
American, 1870-1953
Deer Isle—Marine Fantasy, 1917
watercolor, 19¼" x 16"
Purchase, 1966
15,162

62

CLAUDE MONET
French, 1840-1926
Water Lilies
oil on canvas, 29½" x 78¾"
Purchase in memory of Mr. Robert Allerton, 1966
3385.1

GEORGES BRAQUE
French, 1882-1963
Apple
oil on canvas, 19¼" x 25¼"
Gift of the Friends of the Academy, 1941
4952

GASTON LACHAISE
American, 1882 (Paris)-1935 (New York)
Walking Woman, 1922
bronze, 19½" high
Gift of Mrs. Philip E. Spalding, 1941
4956

64

GIORGIO DE CHIRICO
Italian, 1888-
The Great Machine, 1925
oil on canvas, 61½" x 36¾"
Gift of the Friends of the Academy, 1945
309.1

FERNAND LEGER
French, 1881-1955
Abstraction, 1926
oil on canvas, 50½" x 36"
Gift of Mr. Robert Allerton through the
Friends of the Academy, 1945
311.1

DIEGO RIVERA
Mexican, 1886-1957
Flower Seller, 1926
oil on canvas, 35¼" x 43¼"
Gift of Mrs. Philip E. Spalding, 1932
49.1

SIR JACOB EPSTEIN
English, 1880 (New York)—1959 (London)
Shulamite Woman, c. 1936
bronze, 20½" high
Gift of Mrs. Theodore A. Cooke and family,
Mrs. Philip E. Spalding, Jr.,
Mr. Judd Cooke and
Mr. Lloyd Sexton, 1936
4281

HENRI MATISSE
French, 1869-1954
Nude Before Mirror, 1936
pen and ink, 15⁷⁄₁₆" x 20"
Gift of Mr. Robert Allerton, 1952
13,117

68

PABLO PICASSO
Spanish, 1881-
The Three Graces, II, 1929
etching (artist's proof), 12¾" x 7¼"
Purchase, 1966
15,172

YASUO KUNIYOSHI
American, 1893 (Yokohama)—1953 (New York)
Ballet Dancers, 1940
charcoal, 65½" x 39⅛"
Gift of Mrs. Philip E. Spalding, 1948
12,441

ARTHUR DOVE
American, 1880-1946
The Brothers #1, 1941
oil on canvas, 20" x 28"
Gift of the Friends of the Academy, 1947
450.1

HENRI MATISSE
French, 1869-1954
Annelies, White Tulips and Anemones, 1944
oil on canvas, 23⅞" x 28¾"
Gift of the Friends of the Academy, 1946
376.1

KARL KNATHS
American, 1891-
Clam Digger, 1960
oil on canvas, 45¾" x 36"
Purchase, 1965
3371.1

KAREL APPEL
Dutch, 1921-
Landscape, 1959
oil on canvas, 51½" x 77"
Gift of Mr. Joseph H. Hazen, 1966
3435.1

ISAMI DOI
American, 1903-1965
Early Spring, 1960
oil on canvas, 40" x 52"
Purchase from the Women's Committee Fund, 1966
3428.1

74

HELEN FRANKENTHALER
American, 1928-
Sun Frame, 1966
acrylic on canvas, 44" x 104"
Purchase, 1966
3386.1

Primitive Cultures

While the collection of "primitive" art is small, it is an area in which expansion is anticipated. Particular attention will be given to those cultures which lie within or fringe the Pacific basin, and showings of such material occur from time to time in the exhibition schedule. The collection presently contains a sizeable group of Hawaiian objects both from the pre-European contact and American missionary periods: tapas, ranging from large examples to small fragments; containers of wood, coconut and gourd; carved implements, and feather capes and leis. In this context, though not properly in the category of primitive art, mention should also be made of a large collection of Hawaiian quilts, some dating from the early missionary period, and of the Frank C. Atherton Collection of Hawaiian stamps, which is housed at the Academy and made available to students of history and philatelists.

The collection in general, as the illustrations suggest, also contains a sampling of Pacific island art forms, pre-Columbian ceramics and African wood sculpture from various tribal groups.

Hawaiian bark cloth (detail)

STOPPER FOR LIME CONTAINER
New Guinea, pre-European period
wood with shell inlay and grass cord, 16½" high
Gift of Mrs. Philip E. Spalding, 1936
4196

FLUTED BOWL
PARROT-SHAPED TRIPOD LEGS
Colima, Mexico, 300-1250
ceramic, 9¾" high
Purchase, 1957
2294.1

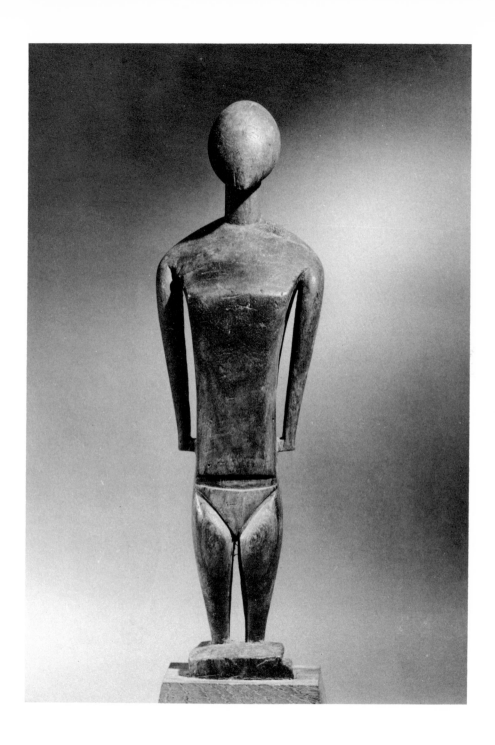

STANDING FIGURE
Micronesian (Nukuoro Island), probably 19th century
wood, 15⁵⁄₁₆" high
Exchange, 1943
4752

MOCHICA STIRRUP JAR
Peru, c. 500 B.C.
ceramic with painted decoration, 11¼" high
Gift of Mrs. Theodore A. Cooke, 1934
3990

80

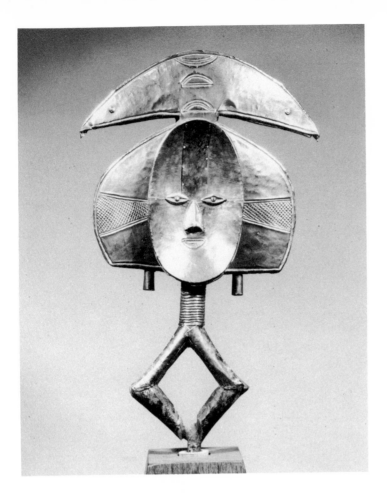

FUNERARY FIGURE
Bakota style, Gabun, Africa
wood covered with sheets of brass and copper, 25" high
Purchase, 1936
4265

STANDING MALE FETISH FIGURE
Bateke style, Western Belgian Congo
wood, 13" high
Purchase, 1958
2456.1

Oriental
Collections

Oriental Collections

Building on the initial donations of Mrs. Charles M. Cooke, the oriental wing of the Academy has been enriched over the years through purchase and gift to a point where it may now be considered on of the more significant collections of its kind in the western world. Mrs. Cooke's gifts included such important works as a pair of screens by Kano Koi, a set of Chinese temple pillars, a 10th century South Indian Dvarapala of granite and some choice pieces of Chinese and Korean ceramics.

Scores of generous patrons have helped in the creation of the oriental collections, notably the late Robert Allerton, whose deep and abiding interest in Japanese art made it possible for the Academy to acquire outstanding examples of Japanese wood sculpture, painting and applied arts. Chinese art is likewise included in the Allerton acquisitions. The Wilhelmina Tenney Memorial Fund also has made it possible to assembly a group of objects remarkable both for range and for quality, perhaps the most famous work being the beautiful ink painting by the Chinese master, Hung-jen; in Japanese art a metalwork basket of the type called *keko* is an important acquisition, as are screens by Taiga and Kiitsu.

Since 1952 numerous masterworks have entered the Academy through the generosity of Mrs. Carter Galt. Her donations in western art have been noted elsewhere. In oriental art there can be singled out the Japanese wood *apsaras* of the Heian period, the figure paintings by the Ming artist, Chou Ch'en, a handscroll of great importance by Wen Cheng-ming and other fine works.

That the Academy is recognized as a noteworthy center for the study of Chinese ceramics is due in large measure to the collection given by the late Edgar J. Bromberger of New York. Significant contributions in the field of Chinese and Korean ceramics have also been made by Lieutenant General (USAF, Retired) Oliver S. Picher and the late W. Damon Giffard.

The James A. Michener Collection of approximately five thousand Japanese prints, ranging from the primitives to the moderns and now housed in the Academy of Arts, is a particularly noteworthy group of both masterworks and study materials.

The following donors have also made substantial contributions to the oriental collections: Mr. Philip E. Spalding and the late Mrs. Spalding, Mr. and Mrs. Theodore A. Cooke, Mr. John Wyatt Gregg Allerton, Mrs. Robert P. Griffing, Jr., the late Mr. and Mrs. Walter F. Dillingham, Mr. Henry G. Lapham, Mr. Robert Lehman, the Martha Cooke Steadman Acquisition Fund and the Hui Manaolana.

China

The richness and quality of the Chinese collections of the Honolulu Academy of Arts are the result of a systematic and dedicated effort over the years.

The Bronze Age in China is illustrated by a small but select group of ritual vessels, sculpture, jade and examples of applied arts. An important object not illustrated is a fragment of a large marble vessel in pure Shang style.

Chinese Buddhist sculpture is exemplified by some works of great quality. Perhaps the most important is a Sakyamuni Buddha over 59 inches tall in seated position. Its style indicates a 7th century date. Another famous piece is the portrait of a seated Buddhist priest made of lacquer and dated in accordance with 1099 A.D.

The ceramic collection is remarkable both for breadth and quality. There are excellent examples ranging in date from the Bronze Age through the Ch'ing Dynasty.

Mrs. Cooke's initial gifts included a number of Chinese paintings, but the crowning jewel was "The Hundred Geese" handscroll. Other outstanding paintings were subsequently added, and today it is undoubtedly this section of the Chinese wing which draws the most interest in world-wide terms. The fame of the painting collection rests primarily on its Ming and Ch'ing masters. In addition to "The Hundred Geese" scroll, at least three other works are generally accepted as masterpieces of the first rank: Wen Cheng-ming's handscroll of "Seven Thuja Trees," "Episodes from the Life of T'ao Yüan-ming" by Ch'en Hung-shou, and "The Coming of Autumn" by the monk-painter Hung-jen.

Two of the galleries devoted to Chinese art are graced by some fine pieces of Ming furniture. In the textile collection are examples of tapestry *(k'o-ssu)* and robes. Equally interesting are some unusual pieces of lacquerware dating in time from the Warring States period to the Ch'ing Dynasty.

87

Chinese textile (detail)

RITUAL VESSEL, KUEI
Shang Dynasty, c. 11th century B.C.
bronze, 7" high
Wilhelmina Tenney Memorial Collection, 1967
3487.1

RITUAL VESSEL, TING
Shang Dynasty, 11th century B.C.
bronze, 9¼" high
Purchase, 1940
4838

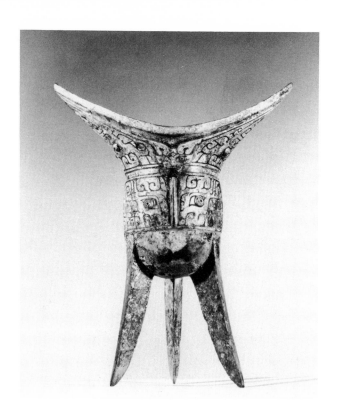

RITUAL VESSEL, CHIO
Shang Dynasty, c. 11th century B.C.
bronze, 8¼" high
Wilhelmina Tenney Memorial Collection, 1966
3414.1

RITUAL VESSEL, TING
Shang Dynasty, 11th century B.C.
bronze, 10⅛" high
Purchase in memory of
Mrs. Charles M. Cooke, 1967
3473.1

90

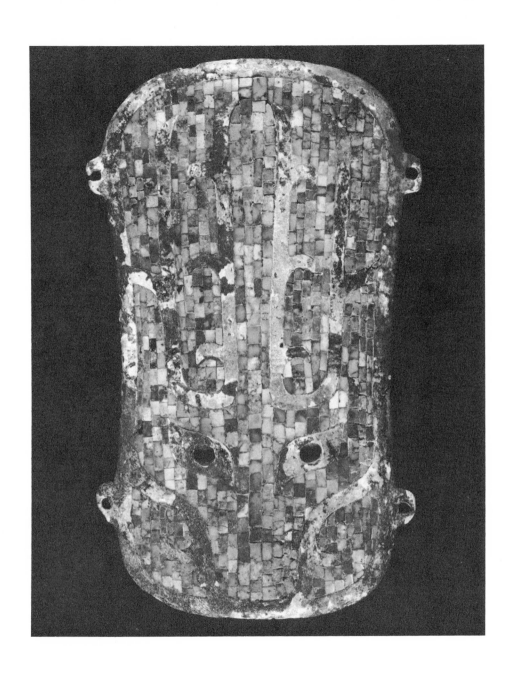

PLAQUE
Shang Dynasty, c. 11th century B.C.
bronze with turquoise inlay, 6½" high
Purchase in memory of Mr. Yozo Nomura, 1967
3453.1

FITTING WITH IBEX HEAD TERMINAL
10th century B.C. (?)
bronze, 13¹³⁄₁₆″ long
Gift of Mrs. Philip E. Spalding, 1939
4784

92

SEATED MAITREYA FROM LUNG-MEN
6th century
stone, 25" high
Gift of Mrs. Calter Galt, 1954
1915.1

TS'UNG (EARTH SYMBOL)
Late Chou Dynasty, 6th-5th century B.C.
nephrite jade (partially calcified), 6¼" high
Acquired through gifts from Mrs. Charles C. Spalding,
Mr. J. Lionberger Davis and Mr. Arthur Wiesenberger, 1967
3503.1

94

SEATED BUDDHIST PRIEST
dated 1099
lacquer, 17½" high
Purchase, 1939
4818

JAR, YÜEH WARE
6th-7th century
stoneware, 7½" high
Gift of Judge Edgar J. Bromberger, 1954
1986.1

SAKYAMUNI BUDDHA
7th century
stone, 59½" high
Gift of Mr. Robert Allerton, 1959
2564.1

ROUND BOX WITH COVER, YÜEH WARE
10th century
stoneware, diameter: 5½"
Gift of Judge Edgar J. Bromberger, 1954
1990.1

EWER
10th century
stoneware, 13⅜" high
Gift of Miss Helen Kimball, 1963
3031.1

EWER
Ming Dynasty, early 15th century
porcelain with decoration in underglaze blue, 10¼" high
Gift of Mrs. Robert P. Griffing, Jr., 1960
2786.1

TRADITIONALLY ATTRIBUTED TO MA FEN
12th century, but possibly by a master of
the 14th-15th century
The Hundred Geese (detail)
ink on paper, painting proper 14" x 15' 3"
Gift of Mrs. Charles M. Cooke, 1927
2121

PALACE VASE
Ch'ing Dynasty, 18th century
porcelain, 27" high
Gift of the family of Mrs. Charles M. Cooke in
commemoration of her 100th birthday, 1953
1799.1

LIU CHÜEH
1410-1472
Landscape, 1438
fan painting, ink on gold paper, 20¼" wide
Gift of Mrs. Carter Galt, 1957
2309.1

WEN CHENG-MING
1470-1559
The Seven Thuja Trees (detail), 1532
ink on paper, painting proper 11¼" x 11'11"
Gift of Mrs. Carter Galt, 1952
1666.1

TRADITIONALLY ATTRIBUTED TO WANG WEI
8th century, but probably by a master of
the 16th-17th century
Clearing after Snowfall (detail)
ink and color on paper, painting proper 11" x 14'8"
Gift of Mr. Robert Lehman, 1960
2725.1

CHOU CH'EN
c. 1450-c. 1535
Street Characters (detail), 1516
ink and light color on paper,
painting proper 12⅜" x 96½"
Gift of Mrs. Carter Galt, 1956
2239.1

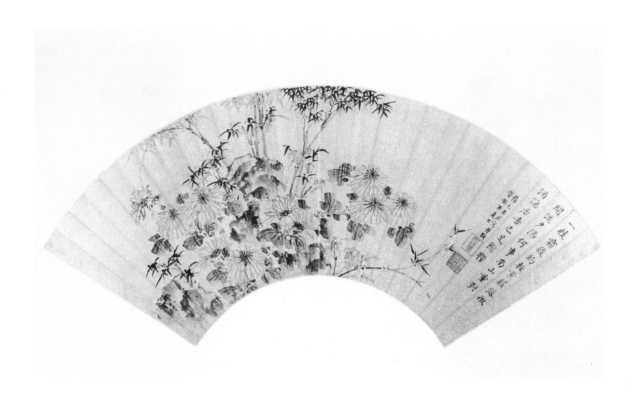

HSÜEH WU
1564-c. 1637
Chrysanthemum and Bamboo, 1633
fan painting, ink on gold paper, 22½" wide
Gift of Mr. Jean-Pierre Dubosc, 1957
2312.1

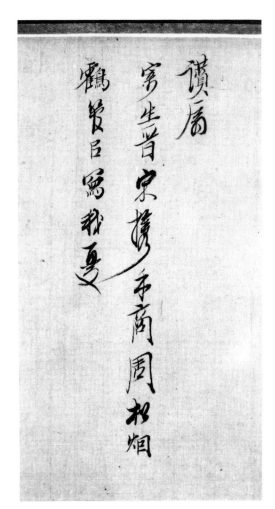

CH'EN HUNG-SHOU
1599-1652
Episodes in the Life of T'ao Ch'ien (details of
calligraphy), 1650
ink and light color on silk, painting proper 12" x 10'1"
Purchase, 1954
1912.1

HUNG-JEN
17th century
The Coming of Autumn
ink on paper, painting proper 48" x 25"
Wilhelmina Tenney Memorial Collection, 1956
104   2045.1

CH'EN HUNG-SHOU
1599-1652
Album Leaf for Yü
ink and color on silk, 10⅛" x 11½"
Purchase, 1966
3420.1

WANG HUI
1623-1717
Landscape in the Manner of Chü-jan (detail), 1696
ink and light color on paper, painting proper 12½" x 13'10"
Martha Cooke Steadman Acquisition Fund, 1960
2711.1

HUANG TING
1660-1730
Mountains in Fall, 1697
ink and light color on paper, painting proper 63" x 21"
Purchase, 1952
1671.1

107

Japan

The Academy's Japanese collection is among the most comprehensive in America or Europe, Japanese art having been one of the major preoccupations of the museum's founder as well as of a number of subsequent donors. Perhaps most widely known is the splendid panoply of Momoyama (1568-1614) and Edo (1615-1867) period screens painted on gold backgrounds, which includes recognized masterpieces of the Tosa and Kano schools, especially of the 16th and 17th centuries. The Sotatsu-Korin tradition of Edo decorative painting is also brilliantly represented from its origin to the 19th century.

Buddhist art of Japan is handsomely documented in the Academy by *Yamato-e* handscrolls and hanging scrolls of the later Heian (897-1184) and succeeding Kamakura (1185-1333) and Muromachi (1334-1567) periods, by metal, wood and lacquer sculptures ranging in date from the 8th to the 14th century, and by a distinguished group of ceremonial utensils and decorative arts made of lacquer, metal and textile. The late Heian *keko* here illustrated (page 114) is the equivalent of its National Treasure twin preserved in Japan.

Shinto art also receives strong emphasis in an outstanding group of wood sculptures of the 12th-13th century. An extensive documentation of the textile maker's art, illustrative of a wide variety of techniques, consists both of mounted fragments dating from the 8th through the 19th centuries and of entire costumes.

Chinese-inspired ink painting of the Muromachi and Edo periods is represented by scroll paintings, *fusuma* (sliding panels) and screens. *Ukiyo-e*, or the "art of the floating world," also occupies an important position in the collection, including notable examples in fan, scroll and screen form as well as an extensive representation of woodblock prints by both old and contemporary masters, among which is the James A. Michener Collection previousy mentioned. Edo painting of a more individualizing character and examples of Momoyama and Edo decorative arts—especially lacquer and ceramics —round out the documentation.

109

Japanese textile (detail)

TILE WITH PHOENIX DESIGN
7th century
clay, 10½" x 11¾"
Given anonymously in memory of
Mr. Robert Allerton, 1965
3356.1

KANNON
8th century
bronze, 15½" high
Wilhelmina Tenney Memorial Fund, 1955
2115.1

110

KICHIJO-TEN
early 10th century
cypress wood, 49¼" high
Gift of Mr. Robert Allerton, 1955
2113.1

GYODO MASK
dated 1086
polychromed wood, 8¼" high
Gift of Mr. Arnold Grant, 1961
2999.1

112

APSARAS
12th century
gold lacquered wood, 48½" high
Gift of Mrs. Carter Galt, 1955
2152.1

113

CHAPTER 454 OF THE MAHAPRAJNAPARAMITA SUTRA
frontispiece and portion of text, 12th century
gold and silver on blue paper, 10⅛" x 32'
Robert Allerton Fund, 1965
3338.1

114

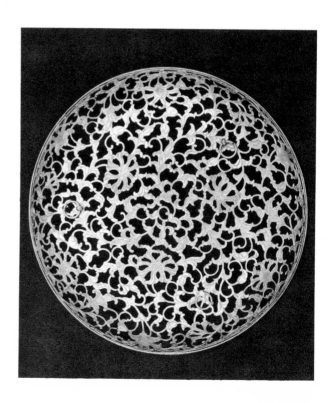

JIZO
12th-13th century
lacquered wood, 48" high
Gift of Mrs. Theodore A. Cooke in memory of
Arthur Hyde Rice III, 1959
2565.1

CEREMONIAL FLOWER BASKET, KEKO
12th century
bronze, gold and silver plated
diameter: 11⅜"
Wilhelmina Tenney Memorial Fund, 1955
2114.1

ATTRIBUTED TO FUJIWARA NOBUZANE
1176-c. 1268
The Poet Mitsune Oshikochi
ink and slight color on paper, 12⅝" x 18⅞"
Wilhelmina Tenney Memorial Fund, 1961
2976.1

SHINTO DEITY
12th-13th century
wood, 44¼" high
Gift of Mr. Robert Allerton, 1964
3311.1

117

KONGO ZUISHIN BOSATSU
13th century
ink on paper, 43⅛" high
Gift in memory of Mr. Langdon Warner
by various donors, 1956
2201.1

BUDDHIST CEREMONIAL TRAY, SESSO-BAKO
13th century
lacquered wood with bronze fittings
14⅛" long
Gift of Mr. John Wyatt Gregg, 1955
2126.1

118

KOBO DAISHI GYOJO E-MAKI (detail of calligraphy)
13th century
ink on paper, 13" x 15"
Gift of Mr. Robert Allerton, 1952
1689.1

COSMETIC BOX, TEBAKO
13th century
lacquer fitted with interior tray
10" long
Purchase, 1966
3418.1

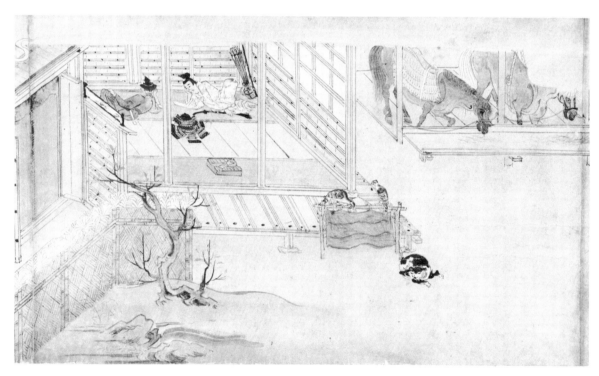

KOBO DAISHI GYOJO E-MAKI (detail)
13th century
ink and color on paper, 13" x 24'1⅝"
Gift of Mr. Robert Allerton, 1952
1689.1

KONIN SHONIN E-DEN (fragment)
13th century
ink and color on paper, 13⅝" x 22"
Gift of Mr. John Wyatt Gregg, 1961
2824.1

JIZO
13th century
lacquered wood with bronze halo, 34" high
Gift of Mr. Yozo Nomura, 1930
2965

122

PAIR OF SLIDING DOORS, FUSUMA
16th-17th century
ink on paper, 71" x 108"
Gift of Mr. Yozo Nomura, 1947
556.1

KANO KOI
c. 1569-1636
Birds and Flowers (detail from a pair of six-fold screens)
ink and color on gold paper, 62" x 23'10"
Gift of Mrs. Charles M. Cooke, 1929
4149, 4150

ENTERTAINMENT NEAR KIYOMIZU TEMPLE
(one panel of a two-fold screen)
16th century
ink and color on gold paper, 64½" x 73½"
Gift of Dr. and Mrs. Ray R. Reeves, 1960
2785.1

HONAMI KOETSU (1558-1637) and
NONOMURA SOTATSU (flourished early 17th century)
Selected Poems from the Wakan Roeishu
ink on silk with background designs painted in gold, 12" x 35'4"
Gift of Mr. and Mrs. Theodore A. Cooke in memory of
Elizabeth Cooke Rice, 1967
3502.1

OGATA KORIN
1658-1716
Blossoming Plum Spray
ink and color on gold paper,
9¼" high
Purchase, 1962
3009.1

126

IKENO TAIGA
1723-1776
Landscape (detail from a pair of six-fold screens)
ink on paper, 67" x 23'9"
Wilhelmina Tenney Memorial Fund, 1964
3299.1, 3300.1

YOSA BUSON
1716-1783
Bird of Prey on Rock, pair of cabinet doors
ink and color on gold paper, 24⅜" x 23½"
Gift of the Hui Manaolana, 1962
3066.1

Wild Flowers (detail from a two-fold screen)
17th century
ink and color on gold paper, 63¾" x 71½"
Robert Allerton Fund, 1966
3377.1

128

UTAGAWA TOYOKUNI
1769-1825
Portrait of the Actor Matsumoto Koshiro IV
color woodblock print, 15" x 10"
C. Montague Cooke Jr. Fund, 1951
13,065

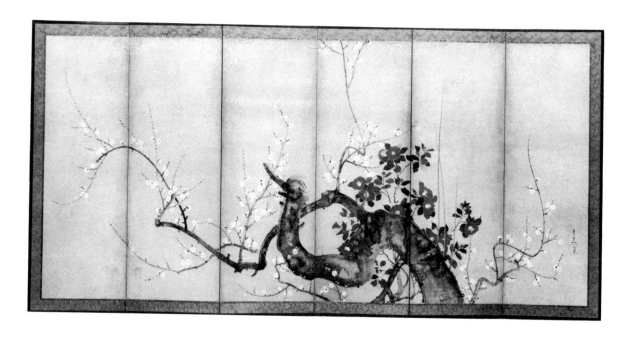

SUZUKI KIITSU
1795-1858
Flowering Plum and Camellia, six-fold screen
ink and color on paper, 63½" x 10'9"
Wilhelmina Tenney Memorial Fund, 1966
3378.1

CHOBUNSAI EISHI
1756-1829
Courtesan Preparing for Bed
color woodblock print, 14¾" x 10"
Gift of Mr. James A. Michener, 1954
13,425

Korea

Korean art is best known in the western world in its ceramic manifestations, and it is in this area that the Academy's Korean collection is the most distinguished. One of the few comprehensive collections of its type outside the Far East, it documents the broad range of Korean stoneware and porcelain from the period of the Three Kingdoms (in the main, Silla vessels of the 5th-6th century) through the Yi Dynasty (1392-1910), with a strong emphasis on the splendid celadons of Koryo Dynasty date (918-1392), a number of which are recognized masterpieces of their kind familiar to connoisseurs of oriental art throughout the world.

In the Academy, students can also find a large collection of sherd material from the most notable Koryo kiln sites and specimens from Yi sites as well. One of the pioneering efforts of its kind anywhere in the world—the nucleus of the collection was assembled prior to 1910—the section of Korean ceramics is constantly being refined and enhanced. In addition, the museum also possesses Korean scroll and screen paintings of both Buddhist and secular subject matter and an important group of Yi Dynasty lacquers, as well as bronze vessels characteristic of both Koryo and Yi manufacture. Representing the lastest aspects of Yi art are typical specimens of furniture and brassware. On occasion the education department arranges special exhibitions of Korean life and culture to recreate the atmosphere of a typical Korean domestic interior.

Korean inlaid lacquer table (detail)

EARRINGS
5th-6th century
gold, 3½" long
Gift of Mrs. Robert P. Griffing, Jr., 1966
3401.1

134

BOWL
12th century
celadon, diameter: 5⅛"
Gift of Lieutenant General (USAF, Retired) Oliver S. Picher, 1955
2053.1

BOWL STAND
12th century
celadon, diameter: 7¼"
Gift of Mrs. Robert P. Griffing, Jr., in memory of
Mr. Walter Damon Giffard, 1966
3434.1

EWER
12th-13th century
inlaid celadon, 6½" high
Gift of Mrs. Charles M. Cooke, 1927
101

SPRINKLER
12th-13th century
bronze, inlaid with silver, 14" high
Gift of Mrs. Alice Spalding Bowen, 1960
2690.1

136

JAR
18th century
porcelain with underglaze designs in
blue and red, 14¾" high
Purchase, 1963
3140.1

ATTENDANT AT A BUDDHIST ALTAR
19th century
polychromed wood, 30" high
Gift of the Charles M. and Anna C. Cooke Trust, 1928
2668

South Asia and the Middle East

Because of a traditional emphasis on the arts of North Asia, the representation of the rest of Asia in the Academy's collections is limited. There are, however, some examples of the art of Greater India and Southeast Asia, mostly in the fields of stone sculpture, textiles, metalwork and decorated manuscripts. The collection of Filipino laces is probably among the most extensive in any museum in the western world.

Middle eastern art in the museum is limited to Islamic art, especially Persian ceramics of the 10th to the 16th centuries and miniature painting primarily of the 16th and 17th centuries, together with a small but fine collection of Persian and Turkish textiles of the 16th, 17th and 18th centuries. The extensive collection of embroidered textiles of the Middle East and the Greek Islands given by Miss Henrietta Brewer in 1933 is a rich source for study and research in this field.

Indian embroidery (detail)

HEAD OF A WOMAN
Hadda, Afghanistan, 3rd-5th century
stucco, 7" high
Gift of Mrs. Carter Galt and
Mr. Robert Allerton, 1957
2292.1

DVARAPALA
Indian, 10th century
granite, 36" high
Gift of Mrs. Charles M. Cooke, 1930
3017

140

BOWL WITH CARVED DECORATION
Persian, 11th-12th century
glazed earthenware, diameter: 6⅜"
Wilhelmina Tenney Memorial Collection, 1962
3070.1

DECORATIVE TILE
Persian, 13th century
glazed earthenware, 7⅞" high
Wilhelmina Tenney Memorial Collection, 1960
2719.1

142

TILE FROM A PRAYER NICHE (MIHRAB)
Persian, 13th century
glazed earthenware, 27½" high
Wilhelmina Tenney Memorial Collection, 1959
2611.1

POLYCHROMED TEXTILE FRAGMENT
Persian, 17th century
velvet, 49" long
Robert Allerton Fund, 1963
3156.1

ILLUSTRATION FROM *The Book of Kings*
Persian, 16th century
color and gold on paper, 10⅞" x 6"
C. Montague Cooke Jr. Fund, 1962
14,856